Famous SHIPS OF THE CLYDE

Jack Webster

PS WAVERLEY

Built by A & J Inglis, Pointhouse, Glasgcw for the London & North Eastern Railway Company
Launched on 2 October 1946 and now the world's only sea-going paddle-steamer
Gross tonnage – 693; Length – 235.5 feet; Beam – 30 feet; Speed – 18.5 knots (maximum), 14 knots (cruising)

NARRATIVE BY JACK WEBSTER

PUBLISHED BY

FOREWORD BY DR JOHN BROWN

ARTWORK BY DUGALD CAMERON

THE GLASGOW ROYAL CONCERT HALL

First published in Great Britain in 1993 by
The Glasgow Royal Concert Hall
2 Sauchiehall Street
Glasgow G2 3NY

ISBN 0 9522174 0 6

A catalogue record for this book is available from the British Library

Design and production by Alan Carlaw

Typeset by Squadron Prints Ltd, Giffnock, Glasgow
Printed by Elpeeko Ltd, Lincoln

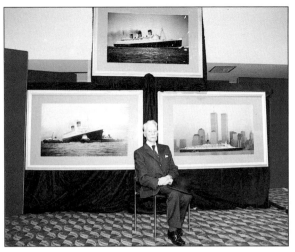

(Photograph by Ian Duffy)

Foreword
by
Dr John Brown
Formerly Managing Director of John Brown & Company Limited, Clydebank

From a Comet to a Queen, from the amazement greeting the arrival of a new form of steam-powered passenger transport on the Clyde to the admiration, over a century later, for three majestic Royal Ladies destined to sail the much wider waters of the seven seas, this collection of photographs illustrates the range and variety of vessels claiming the proud description of "Clyde Built".

It is fashionable today to speak of the need for entrepreneurial skills but the reputation of the Clyde has been created over a century and a half by entrepreneurs such as Robert Napier, John Elder, James and George Thomson and the "family firms" like Scott, Stephen, Connel, Yarrow, Denny, Lithgow, who showed initiative and commercial courage in times of varying prosperity and depression. Their outlook was shared by the larger companies who evolved, John Brown, Fairfield, Beardmore, and who contributed a major share of the naval and merchant tonnage built on the river.

Their achievements were only possible by virtue of the dedication and craftsmanship displayed, often in appalling conditions, by that hardy breed of men, shipbuilders and engineers, on whom the fame of the river ultimately depended.

This record of a selection of their products affords some justification for "the pride of the Clyde".

John Brown

PS COMET

In the early part of the 19th century a Helensburgh engineer called Henry Bell began to pursue the idea that the steam engine, perfected by James Watt from across the Clyde at Greenock, could be used to propel ships. Curiously, Watt himself saw no future for the steamship and rather dampened enthusiasm.

But Bell, who had been an engineer in Glasgow and was helping his wife to run a hydropathic hotel in Helensburgh, was not to be put off. In 1811 he went to see John Wood, a Port Glasgow shipbuilder, who agreed to build a 45ft wooden paddle steamer which became famous around the world as the *Comet* (It was named after Halley's Comet, the heavenly body which appeared in the sky during building).

The *Comet* became known as the mother of the British steamship, so small that you could have fitted her 25 times along the deck of the *Queen Elizabeth*, and could be said to have created a shipbuilding industry in Britain.

Bell was not counted a great maritime engineer nor much of a businessman; he was just someone who pursued a dream. Indeed not even the dream was his own. Another Scots engineer, William Symington from Leadhills, had in fact built the first commercial steamship in the world, the *Charlotte Dundas*, but it so damaged the banks of the Forth and Clyde Canal that it was withdrawn (Nobody seems to have thought of trying it in open water).

So Bell stepped in, created his *Comet*, ran it for passengers between Glasgow, Greenock and Helensburgh but found it too small to be viable. By the time he lengthened it by 20ft, more astute businessmen had moved in and, within a few years, he had more than 20 competitors. So he opened up another route, through the Crinan Canal to Oban and onwards to Inverness.

Henry Bell tried to interest the Admiralty in his idea of steam but only Lord Nelson had the vision to support him and to forecast success. The Americans were not so slow. They dispatched an American-Scot, Robert Fulton, to see what Bell was up to. Open with his plans and generous with his welcome, Bell had his brain successfully picked before Fulton went hotfoot back to America, built a steamship of his own, gained exclusive rights on the Hudson River – and made a fortune.

All too typical of Britain with its inventors, Henry Bell was still trying to raise the money and *Comet* came five years after Fulton's ship, making him no money at all.

Returning to Glasgow from Inverness one December day in 1820, *Comet* was lifted on to the rocks at Craignish Point, near Oban, and wrecked. Her engine was salvaged and used to drive machinery at a brewery. But in 1862 it was rescued and bought by that great engineer, Robert Napier, who presented it to the Science Museum in London, where it remains.

Bell built another *Comet,* which perished. Poor, depressed and in failing health, he was voted a pittance by the Government (How much better if they had supported him in the first place). Friends gathered £500 as a testimonial and the Clyde Navigation Trust gave him an annuity.

Henry Bell died in 1830, aged 63, and is buried in the churchyard at Rhu, near Helensburgh.

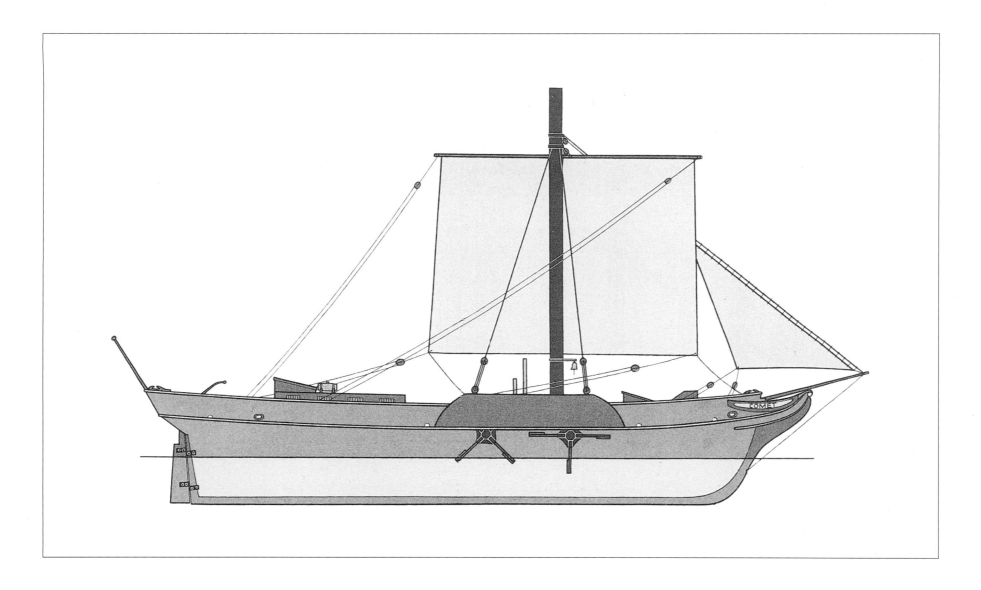

PS COMET

Built by John Wood, Port Glasgow for Henry Bell, Helensburgh
Launched on 24 July 1812
Gross tonnage – 21.5; Length – 44 feet; Beam – 11.25 feet; Speed – 6 knots

HMY BRITANNIA

Yacht racing in Britain was in the doldrums towards the end of the 19th century when suddenly it received a shot in the arm to revive it. That event was the decision of HRH The Prince of Wales (later to be King Edward VII) to order a rather special yacht from Henderson's yard in Partick, Glasgow.

The great genius of yacht-building in those days was G L Watson of Glasgow, whose firm still exists a century later. The royal yacht which he designed for the future king was the *Britannia*, which turned out to be the fastest in the world, destined to collect an incredible 350 first prizes from 635 races. This large, black-hulled cutter carried no less than 10,000 sq.ft. of sail.

She was launched on 20 April 1893 by Mrs Henderson of the Partick yard and was soon heading south for the Thames.

When King Edward VII died in 1910 the *Britannia* passed to his son and successor, King George V, himself a keen sailor and yachtsman. He and Queen Mary would be found cruising round the coast in the company of two of their sons, the young Duke of Windsor and the future King George VI, both about to embark on naval careers and gaining valuable first-hand experience.

The *Britannia* continued on her remarkable course and even after 30 years still reigned supreme in the yachting world. King George V had said: "As long as I live I will not own any yacht other than *Britannia*."

When he discovered that none of his sons really shared his enthusiasm for sailing the yacht he made it known that, after his death, he wanted it scuttled. In his love of the vessel he was said to have been like a schoolboy home on holiday.

He died in January 1936 and in the weeks of mourning the *Britannia* lay largely forgotten in her winter berth. But her gear was sold off in the summer of that year and Britannia was soon on her last journey, to St Catherine's Point, south of the Isle of Wight. There the accompanying cavalcade stopped and in the darkness an explosive was fired into her hull. She sank quietly, her lead keel taking her to the bottom.

There she has lain for nearly 60 years but reports in the 1990s showed that she was still in good condition. There were even reports that she could sail again. All this prompted moves to have her raised and replicated on the Clyde, under the supervision of her original architects, G L Watson, who remain in business at the Kelvin Science Park, Glasgow.

Meanwhile, a superb model of the *Britannia* has gone on permanent display at Glasgow Royal Concert Hall, the work of distinguished model-maker Andrew Short of Pollokshields. Its arrival was a highly suitable way to mark the centenary of that early royal *Britannia* which so captured the public imagination.

HMY BRITANNIA

Built by D & W Henderson, Partick, Glasgow for the Royal Navy
Architects: G L Watson of Glasgow – Launched in 1893
Gross tonnage – 221; Length – 124 feet; Beam – 23 feet

CUTTY SARK

The *Cutty Sark*, whose name was inspired by Scotland's national bard,lies proudly today in her own special dock at Greenwich in London, declared a national monument as the sole survivor of those old sailing ships known as clippers.

She was built in 1869 at Dumbarton (Denny's completed her after Scott and Linton went bankrupt), to the order of a retired sea captain, Jock "White Hat" Willis, who had made a fortune on the China run. She was 216 ft long, with a 35 ft beam and her net tonnage was 918.

Willis had one particular purpose in mind – to outpace the *Thermopylae*, built in Aberdeen a year earlier and hailed as queen of the clippers.

For a Scots Presbyterian, he caused surprise with his choice of name. It came straight from Robert Burns's *Tam o' Shanter*, from the fleet-footed witch called Nannie, whose scanty garment was known as a cutty sark. Indeed her pursuit of *Tam o' Shanter's* mare, clutching at its tail, became the figure-head of Willis's clipper.

It was 1872 before *Cutty Sark* faced *Thermopylae* on a straight test from Shanghai, having loaded their cargoes and set out on the same June day.

By early August the *Cutty Sark* was reckoned to be several hundred miles ahead but in heavy seas she lost her rudder and Captain Moody was delayed ten days in rigging a replacement. Her time of 122 days from China was still regarded as a feat.

In a fairer contest the following year, the *Thermopylae* still beat the *Cutty Sark,* which tended to have cautious masters.

The truth of it was that the *Cutty Sark* came too late for the heyday of the tea clippers, which had a surprisingly short reign of less than 30 years. The opening of the Suez Canal in the year of the *Cutty Sark's* launching had virtually given the tea trade to the steamers.

Because of the prevailing winds, the clippers couldn't use the canal so that by 1877 they were no longer economical for the tea run. The *Cutty Sark* switched to tramping until the late 1880s, when she found a niche in the Australian wool trade, now turning out to be more than a match for the *Thermopylae*. For ten years she ran the fastest voyages home with wool, via the Horn and now captained by a fine sailor, Richard Woodget.

On the way to Australia in 1893, she showed a clean pair of heels to the P&O steamer *Britannia*, counted the fastest ship in the world.

In 1895, Jock Willis sold his beloved ship to a Lisbon firm and for 28 years it sailed as the *Ferreira*. She had yet another name when she anchored at Falmouth, battered by a storm, only to be identified by Wilfred Dowman, a retired sea captain, who bought her back for Britain.

Restored to her own name, she became a training ship but her future was uncertain after the Second World War. A public appeal, boosted by the interest of the Duke of Edinburgh, secured her future at Greenwich, where she was opened to the public by the Queen in 1957.

Looking once more the tea clipper, the *Cutty Sark* is now one of London's leading attractions for tourists.

CUTTY SARK

Built by Scott & Linton, Dumbarton (completed by Denny) for Captain John Willis of London

Launched on 22 November 1869

Gross tonnage – 963; Length – 212.5 feet; Beam – 36 feet

ASS SHENANDOAH

Of all the ships built on the Clyde, none had a more curious or mysterious history than the *Shenandoah*. It seemed like the stuff of fiction, except that it was even stranger.

The ship was built, innocently enough, at the Kelvinhaugh yard of A Stephen & Sons and launched on 18 August 1863 under the name of *Sea King*. Designed by the great Scottish naval architect John Rennie, she was claimed to be the first screw steamship built on the principle of iron frames and wooden planking. She was also the first steamship specially constructed for the China run, intended to beat the best in bringing back the first tea of the season to London.

But the American Civil War was at its height and, while being fitted out at Finnieston, she attracted the attention of agents for the Federal Government, who were looking for war cruisers.

Meanwhile, however, she was chartered by the British Government to take troops to the first Maori War, after which she sailed from New Zealand to China for the apparent purpose of bringing home the tea.

Now she was being eyed by agents for the other side of the Civil War, the Confederates of the south, and when she headed back to Britain there was an officer of the Confederate Navy on board.

The mystery deepened. Back in London, she took on board a cargo of coal for what look like a voyage to Bombay, without arousing the suspicions of the British Government. Instead, on 16 October 1864, she made rendezvous off Madeira with another ship, which brought her munitions and supplies. The *Sea King* was thus handed over to the Confederate Government, brought under the command of a Lieutenant Waddell – and re-named the *Shenandoah*, after the river in Virginia in whose valley many battles of the war had been fought.

Now, as a Confederate raider without equal, the *Shenandoah* proceeded to chase and capture or destroy the incredible number of 37 enemy ships. On one particular day she ploughed into the midst of 11 New England whaling ships, raised the Confederate flag, despatched armed boats and took possession of the lot. Many of the captains were drunk and some swore their sympathy for the southern cause!

She then boarded the British barque, *Barraconta*, en route from San Francisco to Liverpool, only to be given the news that the southern generals had surrendered. The Confederate Government overthrown, the career of the *Shenandoah* as a warship was over.

She later sailed up the Mersey, under the Confederate flag, and was given the official news that the American Civil War was over. Waddell surrendered his ship, which was handed over to the American Consul by the British Admiralty. After being held by the authorities, the whole crew was released.

The *Shenandoah* was later bought by the Sultan of Zanzibar, rounding off a dramatic career for a ship from Stephen's yard on the Clyde which should have been no more than a straightforward tea clipper.

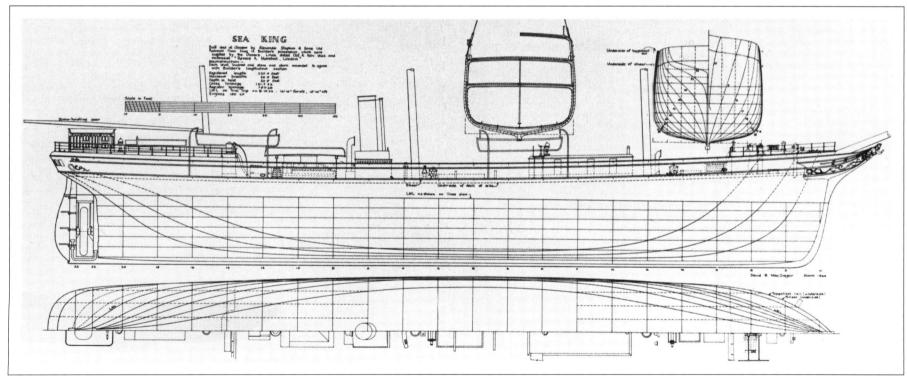

ASS SHENANDOAH
Built by Alexander Stephen & Sons, Kelvinhaugh for the China run
Launched in 1863
Gross tonnage – 1,200; Length – 220 feet; Beam – 36 feet; Speed – 11 knots (registered on trials)

ARIEL and TAEPING

A place in this hall of fame comes to two Clyde-built tea clippers, The *Ariel* and the *Taeping*, because of a memorable and incredible race across the oceans of the world in 1866. As it happened, both ships were built at the Greenock yard of Robert Steele and that challenge race was arranged by their respective skippers, Captain Keay of the *Ariel* and Captain Dowdy of the *Taeping*.

Loaded with their cargoes of tea, the three-masted rigged vessels lined up, the black-hulled *Ariel* with her pink masts and yards and the *Taeping* superbly finished with gingerbread work and brass-inlaid deck fittings, the lighter of the two ships.

Off they set from Foochow on 30 May 1866, up the Min River and out into the China Sea, caught up in strong winds and keeping a constant watch for the pirates who were said to be in league with some of the Chinese pilots.

Ariel led into the Indian Ocean as both clippers took advantage of the strong south-east trade winds and stormed towards the Cape of Good Hope. Into the South Atlantic and *Ariel* found herself nearly 12 hours ahead. Captain Keay decided to sail her directly to St Helena but was slowed up by light winds. Captain Dowdy on the other hand went as close as possible to the African coast and found strong winds which took the *Taeping* across the Equator in a neck-and-neck position.

Onward to the Doldrums, that broad band of calm where sailing ships could lie for months on end, but *Ariel's* wider expanse of sail took her past the Azores still leading by a few hours. Rounding Bishop Rock in the Scillies, *Ariel* was still ahead but *Taeping* hoisted all sail and caught up. In this remarkable encounter, the ships were side by side on the morning of 6 September, just off Dungeness and awaiting pilots to enter London River.

As the first cutter approached, Captain Keay swung *Ariel* round, blocked *Taeping*, picked up the first pilot and was off at such speed that he gained a mile before his rival could recover. Off Deal, both ships had to take on the services of steam tugs for towing up-river and *Taeping* had the luck of the more powerful tug, leading the race past Gravesend.

As the drama built up, the *Taeping* had to anchor to await the tide and Captain Keay came charging up once again. Next day *Ariel* stood off the East India Dock with victory surely in sight. But to the consternation of her captain, she had too much depth to enter and had to await the next tide.

The *Taeping*, on the other hand, went straight ahead to London Docks, got a rope ashore – and was declared the winner. The climax to this astonishing race was that, after 99 days and 16,000 miles across the oceans of the world, these two ships from the same Clyde yard were separated by a mere 20 minutes. It was so close and exciting that the two captains agreed to share the prize money and the bonus.

No wonder the masters, mates and crews were hailed as supermen. No wonder the glory of those sailing ships remains a fascination to the public, who will turn out in their thousands to see the survivors of that genre today.

ARIEL/TAEPING
Built by R Steele & Co, Greenock (both ships) for the China run
Launched in 1865/1863
Gross tonnage – 857/767; Length – 197.4 ft/183.7 ft; Beam – 33.9 ft/31.1 ft

FALLS OF CLYDE

Among the attractions for those who follow the sun to Hawaii is the sight of the *Falls of Clyde*, now the only remaining iron, four-masted sailing ship in the world. For there she lies in Honolulu, a Clyde-built ship which was launched in 1878 and has the added distinction of being an early bulk carrier of oil – one that had no need of the commodity for her own propulsion.

The *Falls of Clyde*, first of nine ships making up the Falls Line – and all of them named after Scottish waterfalls – was built at Russell's yard at Port Glasgow, where she was designed by a young man called William Todd Lithgow. William Lithgow was eventually the sole partner in Russell's shipyard, which became better known to succeeding generations under his own name.

She sailed on her maiden voyage to Karachi in 1879, spending the next 20 years sailing into places like Calcutta, Cape Town, Rangoon, St Helena, Bombay, Auckland, Melbourne and San Francisco.

Seventy voyages later she was sold to the Matson Line of San Francisco, her new owner running up the Hawaiian flag just before the United States annexed the islands. For eight years she carried sugar and passengers to San Francisco and returned with general cargo, livestock and humans. Though sailing ships had already carried oil products in five-gallon containers, it was something different when, in 1907, the *Falls of Clyde* was converted to become a bulk oil tanker.

A young German sailor of poetic tendency, Fred Klebingat, once described catching sight of her gleaming white canvas in the morning sun: "We assembled aft, the captain and his mates, the watch on deck and the watch below, even the cook, just to admire her as she crossed our course astern. Her sleek brown hull was ornamented at the bow with a graceful figurehead, a lady in white, who with unseeing eyes gazed out over the path ahead." Little did young Klebingat know that one day he would be her chief mate. She carried oil throughout the First World War and, after her last voyage in 1922, was converted to a floating oil depot in Alaska.

In 1958 she was due to be sunk to form a breakwater in Vancouver Harbour when up popped the poetic German sailor. When Captain Klebingat saw his old ship in such good order, he went to see Karl Kortum, director of the San Francisco Maritime Museum. But their efforts to find a saviour seemed to have come unstuck when finally they aroused interest in Honolulu. Local newspapers and radio stations joined the campaign, children collected money in cans and, two days before a mortgage deadline, she was saved, to be taken over by the Bishop Museum in Honolulu, where she was restored.

Among those who fell for her graceful lines was Sir William Lithgow, grandson of her designer, whose Scottish yard provided her with 19th century gear. Sir William's son has also worked on her, helping a great lady of the sea to live on.

FALLS OF CLYDE

Built by Russell & Co, Port Glasgow for the Falls Line
Launched in 1878
Gross tonnage – 1,809; Length – 323 feet; Beam – 40 feet; Rig – Four masted full-rigged ship

GLENLEE

The picture of an elegant three-masted sailing ship displayed in the Circle foyer of Glasgow Royal Concert Hall in 1993 – and the news that she had arrived back in the Clyde – sent many a sightseer scampering towards Yorkhill Quay to survey the reality. For there, awaiting restoration, lay the *Glenlee*, the last available Clyde-built sailing ship in the world, rescued by the Clyde Maritime Trust in the drama of a Spanish auction and brought back to the river of her creation for the purpose of permanent display.

The story had begun in 1896 at the Port Glasgow yard of Anderson Rodger and Company, where the *Glenlee* was built as a large steel barque for Sterling and Company of Glasgow. In all truth, she had arrived at the tail-end of her era, when the world was already by-passing commercial sail and the fine-lined clippers were giving way to large iron and steel carriers which would carry maximum cargo under the most economical rig.

In that uncertain climate the *Glenlee* was sold on to Ferguson's of Dundee within two years and, not far into the new century, she was sold again, to R Thomas and Co., managers of the Flint Castle Shipping Company of Liverpool.

Already the name *Glenlee* had been replaced by the *Islamount,* which was to be found on trips to Rotterdam, sailing for Vancouver and down to Peru, Chile and back to Falmouth. Indeed she was all over the world as a bulk carrier.

The First World War offered sailing boats an extended life but the end of that conflict sent many a windjammer to the scrap-heap. The *Islamount* made her last voyage under the Red Ensign in November 1919, sailing from Java to Cette in France with a cargo of sugar.

She was then sold to Italian owners in Genoa and given her third name, *Clarastella,* but that was short-lived. For she was on the move again, this time to Spain, whose government was looking for a naval training ship. She emerged from alterations with yet another name, the *Galatea*, now powered by twin Atlas diesels and at full strength carrying 17 officers, 30 petty officers and 260 ratings and boys. That was in contrast to her days under the Red Ensign when her crew didn't extend beyond 28.

Thus the *Galatea* settled to her training role with the Royal Spanish Navy, which lasted from 1922 till 1969, when she was laid up.

In 1990 she was located by the Clyde Maritime Trust in Seville Harbour and a survey indicated that she was still in a condition worthy of restoration. Mr Hamish Hardie of Glasgow, one of the Maritime trustees, set sail for the rigours of a Spanish auction, the currency problems of which brought some anxious moments of drama.

But he was victorious – and it took £60,000 to survey, buy and insure the old Clyde ship and secure it in Seville Harbour. Nearly 100 years after her birth, the 245 foot vessel was thus towed back to where she started. Her hull was painted at Greenock before she proceeded up to Yorkhill Quay in Glasgow.

The Trust launched a public appeal and embarked on the restoration. In July 1993, Lord Provost Bob Innes of Glasgow gave her back the name with which she had started. The *Glenlee* was home for good.

GLENLEE

Built by Anderson Rodger & Co, Port Glasgow for Sterling & Co, Glasgow
Launched in 1896
Gross tonnage – 1,613; Length – 245.5 feet; Beam – 37.5 feet

PS BRITANNIA

The sturdy little paddle steamer *Britannia*, built on the Clyde in 1840, was the first vessel ever commissioned for Cunard's transatlantic service. It was one of four ships built by Robert Napier of Glasgow for this purpose, though he farmed out the construction of the hulls and the *Britannia* took shape at Robert Duncan's yard at Greenock.

Samuel Cunard had gone against tradition in calling for ships which were "plain and comfortable" and without show. They were certainly plain, as Cunard himself had discovered when he sailed on the maiden voyage from Liverpool to Boston in 1840. On arrival, after 14 days and eight hours, he was entertained at a banquet to celebrate the establishment of a steam postal link between Britain and America.

As to the level of comfort, there could have been no better witness than Charles Dickens, who crossed in 1842. En route to a lecture tour of America, he described his cabin as "an utterly impractical, thoroughly hopeless and profoundly preposterous box." The dining saloon was "a hearse with windows" and the food was "a smoking mess of hot collops followed by a rather mouldy dessert of apples, grapes and oranges."

The weather was appalling and he said a bad winter's night on the Atlantic was impossible to imagine or describe. But he tried. Flung on her side in the waves but springing up again, the ship rolled over till the heavy seas struck her with the noise of a hundred great guns.

"She stops, staggers, shivers, as though stunned, and then, with a violent throbbing at the heart, darts onward like a monster goaded into madness, to be beaten down and battered and crushed and leaped on by the angry sea," wrote Dickens. Thunder, lightning, hail, rain and wind were all in contention for mastery. Perhaps not surprisingly, he did not return by *Britannia*.

The ship made about 40 round trips to America under Cunard before she was sold to the Germans and renamed *Barbarosa*. With her machinery removed, she spent her latter years as a sailing ship of the Prussian Navy before being sunk in 1880 – as a target ship.

Cunard R.M.S. "BRITANNIA."

PS BRITANNIA
Built by Robert Duncan & Co, Greenock for the British & North American RMSP Co
Launched in 1840
Gross tonnage – 1,156; Length – 228 feet; Beam – 34.3 feet; Speed – 10 knots

TSS CARONIA

In the bleak austerity following the Second World War, the *Caronia* came down the slipway of John Brown's yard at Clydebank as welcome evidence that there was still a place for the luxurious liner in an age which had taken on the colour of grey. Indeed the distinguishing feature of the *Caronia* was that she was painted in four shades of green, aimed at reflecting the sun and keeping the ship cooler in tropical regions.

The owners, by now called Cunard White Star Ltd, were making their post-war move into the cruise-line market while retaining the option of using her on the seasonal Atlantic route as well.

So the *Caronia* was launched at Clydebank on 30 October 1947 and came into service in January 1949, sporting a funnel claimed to be the largest ever built for a passenger liner and acting as a sail in high winds.

After a maiden voyage to New York she addressed herself to long cruises, which would be her role for the next 18 years. You would find her on world trips in the early part of the year, moving to the Mediterranean, perhaps crossing the Atlantic a couple of times before heading off to the North Cape and Northern Capitals cruise which was always popular. Then it would be back to the Mediterranean and Black Sea ports before the Caribbean, returning to Southampton for annual overhaul around November.

The *Caronia* was not without her mishaps. In 1958, while on a world cruise, she struck the lighthouse on a harbour breakwater at Yokohama in Japan, plunging it into the sea and incurring damage to her own bow.

She was a fairly costly ship to run, operating in that luxury class where there was at least one crew member for every passenger. As a result, towards the end of the 1950s, she began to lose money and the problem increased into the 1960s. Though once pre-eminent in the cruise business, she was now facing heavy competition from other European countries and was sent for a major refurbishment at Harland and Wolff in Belfast in 1965.

She emerged with a new lido deck and open-air swimming pool as well as much redecoration. After a cruise from New York to the Mediterranean in September 1967, however, her owners brought her back to Southampton and offered her for sale.

She was nearly bought by Domun-Turist of Yugoslavia to be used as a floating hotel at Dubrovnik but that fell through and she was sold to the Universal Line of Panama. Her name was changed twice, to *Columbia* and *Caribia*, and she returned to New York with plans for cruising in the Caribbean.

But nothing came of that either and she was laid up for several years, amid much legal wrangling, until her movable fittings were sold off at an auction in February 1974. Two months later she left New York, taken on tow by a German tug, en route to her graveyard in Taiwan. But she was never to arrive.

In a storm, she was cast on to a breakwater at Guam, where she broke into three parts and sank. The wreckage had to be cleared there and then, proving that there is no limit to the indignity which can attend the last days of a great ship.

TSS CARONIA

Built by John Brown & Co, Clydebank for the Cunard White Star Line
Launched on 30 October 1947
Gross tonnage – 34,183; Length – 715 feet; Beam – 91.5 feet; Speed – 22 knots

TrSS KING EDWARD

The *King Edward*, still remembered by many Scots today because she spent most of her service in the home waters of the Clyde, takes her place in this illustrious company for at least one good reason. She heralded a revolution when she was hailed as the first commercial turbine-driven ship in the world, putting into practice the invention of the famous Irish engineer, Sir Charles Parsons, who had already demonstrated his theory on the experimental ship *Turbinia*.

Parsons wanted to prove the superiority of his steam turbine over the reciprocating engine and this enabled his own company and that of William Denny of Dumbarton to fulfil a longstanding desire to work together. They teamed up with an enterprising steamer-owner on the Clyde, Captain John Williamson, who had an ambition of his own – to offer competition to the Campbeltown and Glasgow Steam Packet Joint Stock Company.

So they formed a syndicate which resulted in the *King Edward* being launched from Denny's yard in 1901. She was fast, smooth and attractive and became such a success that she was overtaken a year later by a larger ship, *Queen Alexandra*.

The *King Edward* was then to be found on the Clyde route sailing via Dunoon, Fairlie and Rothesay to Tarbet, Ardrishaig and eventually to Inveraray. Her presence was to squeeze out the familiar paddleboat, *Lord of the Isles*.

With the outbreak of the First World War she worked as a troopship in the English Channel and was fitted out for hospital work, sailing to the Russian port of Archangel. After the first war she seldom left the Campbeltown route until the arrival of the *King George V* in 1926.

The *King Edward* had her moments of alarm, like the incident of July 1925 when she was rammed off Largs by the *Duchess of Argyll*. Still plying the Clyde waters in the Second World War, she was in collision with the *Lairdsburn*. And a few years later she had her mast snapped off when a tow rope from a tug to another ship lashed across her foredeck.

As part of the nationalised fleet after the war, you would still find her making railway connections on the Clyde coast. Soon after her golden anniversary in 1951, however, she was taken to the breaker's yard in Troon and another great favourite was gone for ever.

Her machinery had still been running as smoothly as ever and, in an age of the noisier diesel, there were plenty of people who mourned the passing of such a quiet and elegant ship as the *King Edward*.

TrSS KING EDWARD
Built by William Denny & Bros, Dumbarton for the Turbine Syndicate
Launched on 16 May 1901
Gross tonnage – 562; Length – 250 feet; Beam – 30 feet; Speed – 20.5 knots

TSMV AORANGI

When the *Aorangi* sailed on her maiden voyage from Southampton to Vancouver in January 1925 she was the largest and fastest motorship in the world. Her origins sprang from the wish of the Union Steam Ship Company of New Zealand to replace their *Aotearea*, which had been lost on war service before it could embark on the Canadian–Australasian route.

The company discussed the possibility of a 16,000-ton steamer with Fairfield's of Govan, who had built a previous ship called the *Aorangi*. This time they were advised by Professor Percy Hillhouse, of the Chair of Naval Architecture at Glasgow University, who was recommending a diesel ship. As well as being an academic, Professor Hillhouse was an architect for the Fairfield yard and he proceeded to design the ship he was proposing. There had been a fashion to reduce funnels to short, squat affairs but Hillhouse went back to two substantial stacks for his diesel ship. She was fitted with four six-cylinder Fairfield-Sulzer engines and had a speed of 18.24 knots.

After that maiden voyage to Vancouver, she settled down to a regular run on the route from Vancouver to Sydney, Australia, operating with the older *Niagara,* which was sunk in 1940.

By 1931 she was under the ownership of the Canadian-Australasian Line in London, a company formed by Canadian Pacific and the Union SS Company to operate the Vancouver-Sydney service. The accommodation was altered in 1938 to reduce the number of first-class passengers and by 1940 she was being altered again for the wartime purpose of troop transport. In 1946, with the war now over, the *Aorangi* returned to passenger service, with her first-class capacity further reduced. But it was not until 1948 that she resumed her familiar route between Vancouver and Sydney, where she operated alone until 1953.

She was then sold for scrap to the British Iron and Steel Corporation and in July 1953, barely 30 years old, she arrived back in the Clyde, to be broken up by Arnott Young & Co, who had established a breaker's yard at Dalmuir, on the site of the once-famous shipyard of the Beardmore company.

TSMV AORANGI
Built by Fairfield, Govan, Glasgow for the Union SS Company of New Zealand Ltd
Launched on 17 June 1924
Gross tonnage – 17,491; Length – 600 feet; Beam – 72.2 feet; Speed – 17 knots

HMS BLACK PRINCE

When the warship *Black Prince* went down the slipway at Robert Napier's Govan yard in 1861 she was the largest vessel ever to have been launched on the Clyde. The event caused keen excitement in Glasgow and was watched by a huge crowd in pouring rain.

But her significance went beyond her size. When the French announced plans to build their famous *Gloire*, the British Admiralty was in the midst of converting its fleet of wooden warships to steam.

Stung into action by the French, it decided on the revolutionary choice of combining armour plating with an iron hull and powerful steam engines. This would make all existing heavily armed ships obsolete but it gave Britain the lead once more, since none could match our ability to build iron steamships.

It did, however, require the expertise of private shipbuilders and engineers and, in 1859, Robert Napier, commonly known as the father of Clyde shipbuilding, was asked to make proposals for a new class of warship, larger and more complex than anything known before.

Napier took up the challenge, made sure his Parkhead Forge could produce the necessary iron forgings and armour plate – and was rewarded with the order for one of Britain's first two "ironclads", to be called *HMS Black Prince*. Before her launching, the Clyde had to be specially dredged to take a vessel of 420ft in length and displacing 9250 tons.

For all his enthusiasm and planning skills, however, Napier made serious miscalculations as to the cost of the project and soon found his tender of £283,000 was far from adequate. It put his company into a perilous position financially.

Like the other new ironclad, *HMS Warrior,* the *Black Prince* had three masts. Sail was required for cruising and where coal was not easily available but she was designed to be fought under steam.

In fact her sea service is hardly a colourful story and included six years as guardship on the Clyde, from 1868 till 1874. She was noted for her ornamentation, including the most artistic figurehead in the British Navy – a 15ft model of her namesake, the Black Prince in his black armour.

In 1878 the ship came under the command of the earlier Duke of Edinburgh, second son of Queen Victoria, with whom she sailed to Canada, as the largest masted battleship to have crossed the Atlantic. This was for the ceremonials of appointing a new Governor General. Her homeward passage, in one of the worst Atlantic winters on record, marked the end of her regular sea service and the *Black Prince* then spent 18 years with the Fleet Reserve at Plymouth.

From there she went to Ireland as a harbour training ship at Queenstown (now known as Cobh) and was renamed the *Emerald* in 1903. She went back to Plymouth with yet another name, *Impregnable III*, before being finally broken up at Dover in 1923.

HMS BLACK PRINCE
Built by Robert Napier, Govan Glasgow for the Royal Navy
Launched on 27 February 1861
Displacement – 9,210 tons; Length – 380 ft; Beam – 58 ft; Speed – 14 knots under steam, 13 knots under sail

TSS ATHENIA

In the gathering clouds of the Second World War the Glasgow-based passenger ship *Athenia* prepared to leave on her regular run to Montreal, picking up more passengers at Belfast and Liverpool before heading round the north of Ireland for the wide Atlantic.

She would be the last passenger ship to leave Europe before the declaration of war on 3 September 1939. With so many ships taken out of service, including the *Queen Mary* at Southampton, there was a mad scampering by Canadians and Americans visiting this country to get back home before trouble broke out.

Glasgow hotels had been filled for days with people speculating that they might land a berth on the *Athenia*. Among others heading for America were some Jewish refugees from Europe.

As the ship edged out of the Prince's Dock on 1 September, past her birthplace at Fairfield's yard and down the river, some passengers leaning over the rails were shocked to hear Clydeside workers shouting at them "Cowards! Cowards!" When she finally struck out for the Atlantic, the Donaldson Line vessel had on board a total of 1,147 people, more than three-quarters of them women and children.

Meanwhile Chamberlain declared war on Germany at 11am that day, by which time the *Athenia's* passengers were thinking they would be clear of possible danger. But the German submarine U.30 was already lurking 200 miles off the Irish coast and, in that early evening of 3 September, when the Athenia's passengers were at dinner, it fired three torpedoes, one of which went straight into the side of the ship.

The first shots of the war had been fired. The first ship was about to sink. The first victims were about to be recorded. The death toll reached 112, the remainder being picked up from lifeboats and many of them brought back to Glasgow. The world was outraged at this early targeting of civilians. Embarrassed Germans blamed Churchill, saying it was his ploy to bring America into the war, and it was not until after the war that their guilt was admitted.

Back in Glasgow, survivors were given a civic reception and entertained by Sir Harry Lauder. A surprise visitor was the young John F Kennedy (his notorious father was then United States Ambassador to Britain), who posed for pictures with American survivors at the Central Hotel.

Thus the *Athenia* took her tragic place in history – the first ship to be sunk in the Second World War. With her sister, the *Letitia*, she had been built at Govan for the Donaldson Line and had quietly plied that route to the St Lawrence from 1923 until the arrival of that unwelcome fame in 1939.

TSS ATHENIA
Built by Fairfields, Govan, Glasgow for the Donaldson Line
Launched on 28 January 1922
Gross tonnage – 13,465; Length – 538 feet; Beam – 66.3 feet; Speed – 16 knots

TSS CONTE ROSSO

The history of the Italian luxury liner *Conte Rosso* illustrates clearly the kind of curious fate which can befall a ship. Ordered by Lloyd Sabaudo of Genoa, she was first laid down at Beardmore's yard in Dalmuir in 1914, a few weeks before the outbreak of the First World War, and was intended for passenger service between Genoa and New York.

In the middle of the war, however, the British Admiralty took over the hull and ordered it to be completed as an aircraft carrier! Thus it took the name of *Argus* and was ready just in time for the end of the war. That ship was later rebuilt for training, served in the Second World War and was finally broken up for scrap at Inverkeithing in 1946.

Meanwhile, after such a false start, the original order was resumed at Beardmore's in 1920 and the *Conte Rosso,* launched in 1921, sailed on her maiden voyage in the following year from Genoa to Buenos Aires. At the first attempt to launch her she stuck 20 feet down the ways and had to be blocked up for the tides of two weeks later. Perhaps the gods were telling her something.

She was the largest mercantile vessel then completed at Dalmuir and was said to surpass all other post-war liners for the luxury of her passenger accommodation. The *Glasgow Herald* waxed eloquent about the ship's interior: "The entrance hall in the first-class public rooms is in the style of the Italian Renaissance in oak and mahogany. Hand carvings, inlaid work, tapestry and stained glass play a part in the general scheme."

The library was in the style of the Tuscany Renaissance, with fifty paintings embodied in the scheme. There was a grand music room and the upper saloon had a dado richly carved and with tooled leather panels. There were large pictures of war episodes in the life of Conte Rosso, after whom the vessel was named.

Italian artists were brought over to Dalmuir to apply their hand to the various fittings and works of art. So the *Conte Rosso* sailed off to a variety of routes, including Trieste-to-Shanghai.

By 1940, however, she had become an Italian troopship and, in the following year, was on her way to Tripoli in a heavily guarded convoy, carrying 2500 soldiers, when she was torpedoed by the British submarine *Upholder* just east of Sicily. There were 800 dead. So ended the chequered life of a ship which had started as a luxury liner at Beardmore's of Dalmuir.

TSS CONTE ROSSO

Built by Beardmore, Glasgow for Lloyd Sabaudo, Genoa
Launched on 10 February 1921
Gross tonnage – 18,017; Length – 591 feet; Beam – 74.1 feet; Speed – 20 knots

SS SERVIA

Apart from the famous *Great Eastern*, that revolutionary ship designed by the distinguished inventor Isambard Kingdom Brunel and said to be 40 years ahead of its time, the Clyde-built *Servia* was the largest ship in the world when she took to the water in 1881. In addition, she was widely regarded as one of the most elegant vessels of her day as she embarked on her role as an Atlantic liner.

She was built for Cunard and launched from the Clydebank yard of J & G Thomson (it later became John Brown's) under the name of *Servia*, though the original intention had been to call her *Sahara*.

A large ship in those days meant a length of 515 feet and a beam of 52.1 feet, conforming to the fashionable Bibby principle that the length should be ten times the beam.

With a crew of 252 and carrying 480 first-class and 500 third-class passengers, the *Servia* cost £256,903 to build in 1881. Apart from her style, she attracted attention because of her innovations. She was fabricated in mild steel and equipped throughout with electric lighting which was not yet common practice in the 1880s.

Cracks discovered in her shaft before trials meant that her maiden voyage to New York was delayed by several weeks but once she settled into her Atlantic routine she was soon being hailed as a tremendous success. At the beginning the Servia had no boat deck and her lifeboats were on projecting skids.

But it was not all plain sailing. She had to be towed into New York in 1891 after her shaft snapped. Then in the following year she collided with the American sailing ship *Undaunted* and, in 1893, she ran down the sailing barque, *A McCallum*.

In her refit of that year her accommodation was updated and she was given a boat deck.

With the Boer War of 1899, the Servia was chartered by the British Government at 21 shillings per ton per month and was used for trooping under the identity of HMT31. By 1900, however, she had resumed her Atlantic crossings to New York, only to be withdrawn a year later and replaced by the *Ivernia*.

She was then laid up and sold off for £15,625, soon to be stripped at Barrow-on-Furness and towed to Preston for demolition. The comparatively short lifetime of many ships comes as a surprise to the layman. From her elegant arrival in 1881, the *Servia's* span was just under 20 years.

SS SERVIA
Built by J & G Thomson, Clydebank for the Cunard Line
Launched on 1 March 1881
Gross tonnage – 7,391; Length – 515 feet; Beam – 52.1 feet; Speed – 16 knots

TSS CITY OF NEW YORK

Though the 19th century passenger was beginning to acquire a taste for speed on the ocean wave, the big shipping lines were still more concerned with out-doing each other in terms of luxury and magnificence. So nothing was spared by the Inman Line in the 1880s when it ordered two transatlantic liners from J & G Thomson of Clydebank.

The *City of New York* was first down the slipway, in October 1888, a ship of elegance and style which was counted among the most beautiful vessels ever built. Above the low superstructure rose three fine funnels while the sense of speed was heightened by the sight of three masts.

Forward of the bridge was a huge glass roof, adding a breathtaking touch to the first-class dining-room. In a balcony overlooking the diners they had installed a pipe organ no less, which served as an accompaniment for divine service.

Taking her place on the Liverpool-to-New York service, she captured the Blue Riband and combined with her sister ship, the *City of Paris*, which was completed seven months later, in the contest for supremacy over the White Star's *Majestic* and *Teutonic*. In the event, none of the four was able to match the performance of the two Cunarders, *Campania* and *Lucania*, when they came on the scene in 1893.

By then, however, the Inman Line was running into the financial difficulties of hard economic times and the ship was sold to the American Line and had her name shortened to the *New York*. Under the new ownership, she plied the route from Southampton to New York for the five years from 1893 until she was called into service for the Spanish-American war, when she became an auxiliary cruiser of the US Navy under the new name of *Harvard*.

Restored to her own name after the war, the *New York* was sent to Philadelphia for a refit, emerging with just two funnels instead of her original three, a change which upset the balance of her contours. Further changes left her without first-class accommodation but she was still plying the Atlantic until America joined in the First World War in 1917, when this stately liner found herself conscripted once more.

This time she became an armed transport ship with yet another name, the *Plattsburg*, and her second mast removed. Resuming the peacetime role in 1919, once more as the New York, she was then laid up in 1920 and sold the following year to the Polish Navigation Company, adapting to new routes from New York to Danzig and the Mediterranean.

Her lifespan ran to 35 years before she was sent to the breaker's yard in Genoa in 1923, by which time she and her sister ship had become true legends of the Atlantic.

TSS CITY of NEW YORK

Built by J & G Thomson, Clydebank for the Inman Line
Launched on 15 October 1888
Gross tonnage – 10,499; Length – 560 feet; Beam – 63.2 feet; Speed – 21 knots

TSS CITY OF PARIS

Coming into service in the spring of 1889, the *City of Paris* was the second of those two large and fast liners which had been ordered by the Inman Line from the Clydebank yard of J and G Thomson.

She ran her maiden voyage from Liverpool to New York and settled more quickly to the role of record-breaker than her sister, the equally luxurious and magnificent *City of New York.* On what was only her second westward crossing she captured the Blue Riband with a record average speed of 19.95 knots and that was followed by a homeward voyage at 20.02 knots.

Ownership became a rather complicated matter with the changing fortunes of the Inman Line, which had run into financial difficulties. Heading for liquidation, the company was taken over by the International Navigation Company, which owned the American and Red Star Lines. The name was the Inman and International Steamship Company and, although the ships continued to fly the British flag, the company was essentially American.

There came a time, a few years later, when the American people were not at all happy about the British flag and Congress passed an Act which enabled the *City of Paris* and the *City of New York* to be transferred to American registry.

Following close upon that, the Postmaster General of the United States accepted the company's tender to carry the American mail, no longer from New York to Liverpool but now to Southampton.

These events of 1893 coincided with the two ships having their names shortened to the *New York* and the *Paris,* now in the ownership of what was known as the American Line, the grand old name of Inman disappearing altogether. A distinctive feature of the *New York* and the *Paris* was a most complete system of watertight bulkheads, both traverse and longitudinal.

While still known as the *City of Paris,* the Clydebank ship came near to disaster in March 1890, when she was moving at full speed not far from the Irish coast. The starboard propeller snapped, with the result that the engine raced and wrecked both itself and the longitudinal bulkhead. The sea connections were so badly damaged that both engine rooms were flooded and the ship had to be towed to Queenstown, rendered out of action for months.

Like her sister, the *Paris* was commissioned in 1898 as an auxiliary cruiser during the Spanish-American War, under the name of *Yale.* By 1901 she was back in service, this time as the *Philadelphia,* and was running on the New York–Liverpool route in the early part of the First World War.

Again like her sister, she was conscripted for the US Navy in 1917, serving as an armed transport, with her second mast removed – and under yet another name, the *Harrisburg.*

Resuming normal service in 1919, as the *Philadelphia,* she was soon to be sold to the New York–Naples Steamship Co. On her first voyage on that route, however, there was a mutiny on board, with the crew making a serious attempt to sink the ship. Such can be the fate of ships which sail innocently out of their cradles in the Clyde.

The ship which had started out as the *City of Paris* was then laid up in Naples and a year later she was taken to the breaker's yard in Genoa, the same graveyard which greeted the *City of New York* in the same year.

TSS CITY OF PARIS

Built by J & G Thomson, Clydebank for the Inman Line
Launched on 23 October 1888
Gross tonnage – 10,499; Length – 560 feet; Beam – 63.2 feet; Speed – 20 knots

TSMV CIRCASSIA

When the passenger-cargo liner *Circassia* went down the slipway at Fairfield's of Govan in 1937, she was the first motorship produced for the Anchor Line.

She was then followed by the *Cilicia* and the *Caledonia,* all three of which gave excellent service. The *Circassia* sailed on her maiden voyage from Glasgow and Liverpool to Bombay in October 1937 and remained on the eastern service until the Second World War. Soon after that maiden voyage, her Anchor Line owners became involved in a unique manner with Scotland's greatest-ever spectacle, the Empire Exhibition at Bellahouston Park, Glasgow. Into the hillside of Bellahouston they built the spectacular Atlantic Restaurant in the shape of the bridge, fore-deck and bow of a ship. It was there that King George VI and Queen Elizabeth were entertained to lunch after opening the exhibition.

On the day war was declared, 3 September 1939, the *Circassia* was in Aden on her way to Bombay. Completing that run, she arrived back in Glasgow in October and, like so many other of her kind, was requisitioned as an armed merchant cruiser before becoming a troopship in 1942.

On a voyage to North Africa she was in the same convoy as the *Cameronia* when that ship was torpedoed. With the convoy under attack from the air, the *Circassia* was credited with having shot down one of the planes. After further trips to North Africa she returned to the Clyde in the spring of 1943 when she was rearmed with anti-aircraft weapons. She was next seen carrying out exercises in assault-landing on the shores of the Firth of Clyde. In June she took on board troops of the First Canadian Division and joined other ships in the Gareloch to prepare for Operation 'Husky', which was the landing on Sicily.

Circassia was having a busy war. Her troop duties took her as far as the familiar port of Bombay before returning to Naples to be detailed for service with US Naval Forces.

In January 1944 she sailed with American forces and took part in the landings at Salerno. When she arrived back in the Clyde in September she had been operational for nearly 15 months. But she was off again to Bombay and twice to Odessa with liberated Russian prisoners-of-war before bringing home British prisoners who had been freed in the Russian advances.

Even in July 1945 she left Glasgow again for the east, putting Indian troops ashore at Morib in the Straits of Malacca. She arrived safely back in the Clyde in March 1946 but it was two years before she resumed her peacetime route to Bombay.

That continued until 1966, when the Anchor Line was planning to end that service after 110 years. It fell to the *Circassia* to make the last passenger sailing. This poignant occasion also rounded off the ship's own career and she was sold for £140,000 to be broken up at Alicante in the spring of that year.

TSMV CIRCASSIA
Built by Fairfield, Govan, Glasgow for the Anchor Line, Glasgow
Launched on 8 June 1937
Gross tonnage – 11,137; Length – 506 feet; Beam – 65.9 feet; Speed – 18 knots

TSMV VICEROY OF INDIA

Poised on the slipway at Stephen's of Linthouse, the gleaming new liner was ready to announce herself to the world as the *Taj Mahal*. A few days before taking to the water in September of 1928, however, the name was changed to the *Viceroy of India*. Whatever the politics of that, this handsome ship became the latest pride of the P & O company, visually impressive and technically special. For this was the first of the large electrically-driven ships on the British register.

The *Viceroy* was expensively furnished in period style, the first-class lounge representing the 18th century and the dining saloon done up according to the French taste of that same period.

Crowning it all, the main smoking room reflected Scotland in the baronial style, complete with a collection of the personal effects of Bonnie Prince Charlie no less. Add to that an indoor Pompeiian swimming-pool and you had a ship with a difference.

She was launched at Linthouse in September 1928 by the wife of the Viceroy of India and sailed on her maiden voyage in the following March, leaving London for Bombay, via Marseilles, Malta and Suez.

Back at Tilbury, she cruised throughout the summer and, on her return to the Indian service, broke the London-Bombay speed record with a time of 16 days, one hour and 42 minutes.

In September 1935, the *Viceroy* tasted high drama off the Portuguese coast when she went to the rescue of passengers from the Cunard-White Star liner *Doric*, which had collided with a French coaster. After a 40-mile dash she took on board 241 passengers, the remainder being saved by the Orient Line's *Orion*.

Thereafter, until the Second World War, she kept out of the headlines, except for a grounding in the Suez Canal in the spring of 1937. Her schedule included cruising to the Atlantic Isles and the northern capitals.

Then she took over the route to India and Shanghai which should have been the role of another famous ship. Instead, the *Rawalpindi*, converted to an armed merchant-cruiser, found herself fighting an heroic battle with the German battle-cruisers *Scharnhorst* and *Gneisenau* between Iceland and the Faroes, a hopeless struggle in which she finally went under with all 270 of her crew. That included Captain Kennedy, father of the writer and broadcaster Ludovic Kennedy.

The *Viceroy* herself was soon en route for the Clyde to be refitted as a troopship and for 18 months she was sailing to Port Said and Bombay.

On 26 October 1942 she left the Clyde in convoy to Algiers, as part of the North African offensive known as Operation Torch. She reached there early on 7 November and three days later was setting out for home. In the early morning of 11 November, however, she encountered a German submarine and was torpedoed. As the engine-room exploded, four of the crew were killed but the 450 others on board were all picked up.

For four hours the *Viceroy of India* struggled to stay afloat but finally slid to her watery grave just 30 miles north of Oran. Another great ship had perished in the Second World War.

TSMV VICEROY of INDIA
Built by Alexander Stephens & Sons, Linthouse, Glasgow for the P & O Line
Launched on 15 September 1928
Gross tonnage – 19,648; Length – 612 feet; Beam – 76.2 feet; Speed – 19 knots

QSS AQUITANIA

Just as the *Queen Elizabeth* would be completed in time for an unintended role in the Second World War, so did the *Aquitania* take her bow on the eve of the First World War.

Her real purpose had been to team up with the *Lusitania* and the *Mauretania* on Cunard's transatlantic service. At a top speed of 24 knots she was slower than either of those ships but she more than made up for it in luxury and elegance, regarded as one of the finest creations ever to leave John Brown's yard.

Launched at Clydebank on 13 April 1913, she set off on her maiden voyage from Liverpool to New York on 30 May 1914, just weeks before the outbreak of the Great War.

Almost immediately converted to the role of auxiliary cruiser, she collided with the liner Canadian and was soon regarded by the Admiralty as too big and vulnerable to be a cruiser.

So the *Aquitania* became a troopship, carrying 30,000 men to the fierce fighting at Gallipoli in 1915. When that campaign went wrong, she was turned into a hospital ship and before the end of the war was also bringing American troops to Europe.

At last, in June 1919, the *Aquitania* settled to her true purpose on the North Atlantic, helping to establish the Southampton – New York route on which she would spend the next 20 years, a great favourite with that glitterati of royalty and Hollywood stars to be seen on old newsreels, disembarking at Southampton.

The prospect of this Clyde-built ship had initially raised apprehension in the Germans, who were then building the 52,000-ton *Imperator*, intended to outdo all rivals on the transatlantic routes. Ironically, the *Imperator* became part of Germany's reparation to Britain after the First World War and joined the *Aquitania* on Cunard's service to America, under the new name of *Berengaria*.

When the *Queen Mary* came on the scene in 1936 she was teamed up with the *Aquitania*. But the life of the latter was due to end with the completion of the *Queen Elizabeth* in the late 1930s.

It was the Second World War which intervened to give her an extended lifetime. Once again she became a troopship and remained in Government service until 1948, having latterly provided cheap fares for GI brides to America and emigrants leaving Britain for a new life in Canada.

When she made her last voyage, from Halifax to Southampton, she had crossed the Atlantic 475 times and covered a total distance of more than three million miles.

Finally, on 21 February 1950, the great old ship headed towards the Clydeside cradle from which she had emerged 36 years earlier. This time, however, her graceful lines were due for destruction – in the breaker's yard at Faslane.

QSS AQUITANIA

Built by John Brown & Company, Clydebank for the Cunard Line
Launched on 21 April 1913
Gross tonnage – 45,647; Length – 901.5 feet; Beam – 97 feet; Speed – 23 knots

QSS LUSITANIA

By the early part of the 20th century luxury travel on the Atlantic was in danger of being dominated by the Germans and the Americans. Seeking to restore British supremacy, Cunard gained financial backing from the Government to build two very similar and splendid liners which could, if necessary, be converted to wartime purpose.

The order for the *Lusitania* went to John Brown's of Clydebank while the sister ship, the *Mauretania,* went to Tyneside.

The *Lucy,* as she came to be known, was first into the water, launched at Clydebank on 7 June 1906, completed by August 1907. Two months later she captured the Blue Riband with a speed of 23.99 knots.

She was, after all, half as big again of anything afloat and was hailed as the wonder ship of her day. (The *Mauretania* came along a few months later and soon captured her sister's speed record).

In an age when horse transport still dominated, it is not hard to imagine the excitement created by this sleek and stately ship, with its four tall funnels.

Cunard chairman Lord Inverclyde had engaged a young Scottish architect, James Miller (he designed the Glasgow Exhibition of 1901) to decorate the interior of the ship and Miller didn't let him down. For example, the first-class dining room rose two decks, with a plaster dome and a high gallery looking down on the open well.

One shipping writer spoke of "the pleasurable hallucination that one is sojourning in the grandest of hotels on land and that the general surroundings are that of no mean city."

Some were more cynical about the level of luxury but Scots writer George Blake, who saw her edging down river to the sea, was moved by the gracious elegance and called it a ship in a million.

When the First World War broke out, the Admiralty decided the *Lusitania* wasn't really suitable as an armed merchant cruiser after all and, instead, she maintained the mail and passenger service between Liverpool and New York.

Therein lay her fate. In the spring of 1915 Germany gave warning in American newspapers that passengers sailing in Allied ships ran a risk in war zones.

The *Lusitania* left New York on 3 May 1915 and was within sight of the Irish coast four days later when Captain William Turner received warning of German submarines. The U–20, under Kapitanleutnant Walter Schwieger, spotted his target, intercepted this mighty ship of the Clyde just off the Old Head of Kinsale, in southern Ireland, and fired a torpedo from 700 yards. It struck the starboard side between the third and fourth funnels – and the great *Lusitania* sank inside 18 minutes, with the loss of 1200 lives.

Schwieger insisted only one torpedo was fired but the Germans had maintained the ship was carrying munitions, which could have explained a second massive explosion.

It was a tragic end to the great *Lusitania*. A fine sailor, Captain Turner faced some close questioning about the disaster but was cleared of blame. Nevertheless he remained bitter about it for the rest of his life.

QSS LUSITANIA
Built by John Brown & Company, Clydebank for the Cunard Line
Launched on 7 June 1906
Gross tonnage – 31,550; Length – 787 feet; Beam – 87.8 feet; Speed – 25 knots

TSS EMPRESS OF JAPAN

The *Empress of Japan*, which left Fairfield's yard in Govan in 1930, was generally acclaimed to be the finest and most luxurious liner ever built for service in the Pacific.

A career in which she sported three different names began with a round voyage on the Atlantic, from Liverpool to Quebec and back to Southampton before she headed for Hong Kong as Canadian Pacific's latest showpiece.

Thereafter she settled to regular runs from Vancouver and Victoria, via Honolulu, to Yokohama and Hong Kong, sharing that trans-Pacific service with other Empresses – Asia, Russia and Canada. That was her role throughout the 1930s, during which she held the speed record for the Pacific.

The *Empress of Japan* happened to be in Shanghai at the outbreak of the Second World War and headed back to Vancouver Island. There she was painted grey, fitted with guns and requisitioned as an armed troopship. In that role she could be found, in May 1940 for example, as part of a rather distinguished convoy from Australia, which included the *Queen Mary*, the *Aquitania, Mauretania, Andes, Empress of Britain* and *Empress of Canada*.

In 1941 she carried troops to Singapore but with the worsening situation in the Far East she returned there the following year to evacuate women and children.

The role of Japan as an enemy now raised the delicate question of her name. So in 1942 she was re-christened the *Empress of Scotland* and continued troopship duty until after the war, having been under attack several times but escaping serious damage.

Released from military service in 1948, the *Empress of Scotland* was switched to Canadian Pacific's Atlantic route, sailing on her first voyage from Liverpool to Quebec, via Greenock, on 5 May 1950.

In the meantime she had undergone many improvements and now catered for 458 first-class passengers and 250 tourist. There were also cruises during winter to the Caribbean, South Africa and South America and in November 1951 she brought Princess Elizabeth and the Duke of Edinburgh home from their tour of Canada.

With the arrival of two new ships, another *Empress of Britain* and the *Empress of England*, Canadian Pacific decided in 1958 to sell their 28-year-old *Empress of Scotland* to Germany's Hamburg-Atlantic Line.

Rebuilt in superstructure, now with two funnels instead of three, she was given her third name, *Hanseatic*, and catered mainly for tourist passengers on the Hamburg-New York route, with cruising in winter.

Sadly it all came to an end on 7 September 1966 when fire broke out while she was berthed in New York. Damaged beyond salvation, she was towed to Hamburg and later scrapped.

TSS EMPRESS OF JAPAN
Built by Fairfield Shipbuilding & Engineering Co, Govan for the Canadian Pacific Railway
Launched on 17 December 1929
Gross tonnage – 26,032; Length – 666 feet; Beam – 83.5 feet; Speed – 21 knots (23 on trials)

TSS EMPRESS OF BRITAIN

The *Empress of Britain,* completed at John Brown's yard at Clydebank in May 1931, was the largest passenger liner ever ordered by the Canadian Pacific Company. In addition, she had a standard of luxury which has possibly never been surpassed.

Most of Canadian Pacific's leading passenger ships had the title of Empress and this one was the second to be called *Empress of Britain,* the first having been launched on the Clyde in 1906.

Now came a bigger version, launched at Clydebank on 11 June 1930 by the Prince of Wales and specifically aimed at capturing business to and from the American Mid-West. The idea was that a speedy voyage from Britain to Quebec and a rail journey to Chicago would have more appeal than sailing to New York.

She was also designed with long winter cruises in mind, when the St Lawrence would be frozen over, so there had to be adaptability for passing through the Suez and Panama Canals and entering ports of all sizes.

The outcome was a ship which stood high out of the water and had three very large funnels, the third of which was just a dummy but was used as a ventilator for the engine-room.

During trials, she reached a speed of 25.5 knots and her first voyage took just over five days from Cherbourg to Quebec. Good speeds were maintained on a remarkably low fuel consumption and she became known for her reliability.

Those winter cruises took the rich and famous around the world and the *Empress of Britain* did indeed capture her share of that American Mid-West market.

Canadian Pacific knew, however, that two ships would be required to provide a more frequent service but their plans in this direction were ruined by the Depression of the 1930s.

The *Empress* soldiered on, incurring the odd mishap, like a collision in the St Lawrence in which three crew members on a collier were killed.

In 1939 she brought the Royal Family home from their tour of Canada before the ship made her last peacetime departure from Southampton – on the day before the outbreak of the Second World War.

Reaching Quebec, she was laid up, painted grey and diverted to carrying troops, her first mission taking her back across the Atlantic with Canadian forces heading for Britain.

With her high speed, she generally sailed without an escort but it was on such a voyage that she met her fate. On the way from Cape Town to Liverpool on 26 October 1940, she was attacked and set alight by a German bomber off the coast of Ireland.

Rescue ships were on the scene and the *Empress* was taken on tow. Two days later, however, she was torpedoed and sunk by a German submarine.

TSS EMPRESS OF BRITAIN
Built by John Brown & Co, Clydebank for the Canadian Pacific Railway
Launched on 28 November 1928
Gross tonnage – 42,348; Length – 760.5 feet; Beam – 97.5 feet; Speed – 24 knots

HMS VANGUARD

The *Vanguard* was Britain's last battleship and has also been described as the greatest, a claim which lacks confirmation, however, if only because she was never really put to the test. The order was placed under the War Estimates but the Second World War had ended before she took to the water. So not a single shot was fired in anger.

Bearing a name which had gained battle honours dating back to the Armada, the *Vanguard* was christened at John Brown's yard at Clydebank by the future Queen, as Princess Elizabeth, on 30 November 1944, when the war still had six months to run.

It was May 1946, exactly a year after VE-day, before she sailed down the Clyde, all 814 feet of her, with a speed of 29.5 knots. She was acclaimed for her handsome appearance and was to gain a reputation as a very good seaboat.

To speed up her completion, the main armament came from guns and turrets removed from two First World War ships, the *Courageous* and the *Glorious*, which were being converted to aircraft carriers.

These 15-inch guns, regarded as necessary but unfortunate, had a maximum range of only 32,100 yards and didn't compare favourably with Germany's *Bismarck*, Italy's *Vittorio Beneto* or France's *Richelieu*.

The overall design of the ship owed much to the *King George V* class, especially in the armoured protection. She had four separate engine-rooms and armour up to 14 inches thick.

Having arrived in peacetime, she sailed with a crew of 1600 and in 1947 conveyed King George VI on a royal tour of South Africa. There followed a spell of Mediterranean service before she became the flagship of the Home Fleet between 1952 and 1954.

In 1955 there was a proposal to convert the *Vanguard* to a guided-missile ship. But that was abandoned because of the cost of conversion and the development of a suitable missile.

From 1956 she was in operational reserve in Portsmouth and her limited life drew to a close with the decision that, rather than creating any more expense, she should simply be scrapped.

Though perhaps not matching the stature of battleships built for the First World War, the *Vanguard* certainly looked like the best that was built for the second war.

Like many another, her demise was witnessed, in 1960, back home in the breaker's yard at Faslane.

HMS VANGUARD

Built by John Brown & Company, Clydebank for the Royal Navy
Launched on 30 November 1944
Displacement – 51,420 tons; Length – 814.5 feet; Beam – 108.5 feet; Speed – 29.5 knots

HMS LANCASTER

If the old-time bustle of the Clyde, with 50 shipyards or more, has given way to a scene of industrial quiet, there is at least no dilution of the quality which that great river invests in its shipbuilding.

Of the handful of yards still existing, Yarrow's of Scotstoun remains a name synonymous with the highest standards of naval shipping. That fact was fully confirmed with the completion of *HMS Lancaster,* launched by the Queen in 1990 and accepted into service in the following year.

In the modern Royal Navy the frigate is the mainstay of the surface fleet, fast, manoeuvrable and capable of scouting ahead of the main fleet. But there is an extra advantage in the Type 23 Duke Class of Frigate, of which the *Lancaster* is the latest example (It was the third of the class to be built at Yarrow's). Compared to similar ships in other navies, this one is heavily armed.

The design was carried out by Yarrow's, in collaboration with the Ministry of Defence, and is a classic example of that fine tradition which has been established between the Glasgow shipyard and the Royal Navy. The *Lancaster* includes all the latest technology in anti-submarine, surface and anti-air warfare and owes some of its novel features to experience gained in the South Atlantic conflict of 1982.

With an overall length of 133 metres and beam of 15 metres, she pursues her primary role of submarine detection with the latest gadgetry on matters like noise reduction. The form of the hull allows full use of the new EH101 Merlin helicopters, and torpedoes. Surface armament includes Harpoon missiles and the ship is defended by such inventions as the vertically-launched Sea Wolf Anti-Missile system. Within her economic space, *HMS Lancaster* still manages to find accommodation for the captain, 16 officers, 57 senior ratings and 111 juniors.

Like many another, *HMS Lancaster* is by no means the first ship to bear the name. The first was an 80-gun vessel built as far back as 1694. As was common at the time, she was rebuilt twice to suit changing needs. A new *Lancaster* joined the fleet in 1797 and saw action against the Dutch and in the capture of Montevideo.

Then came a frigate, which lasted from 1823 until 1864, followed by an armoured cruiser, launched in 1902 and serving until 1919. One of that ship's guns, landed to protect Port Stanley in 1916, was still in position when the Argentinians invaded the Falkland Islands in 1982.

The fifth ship of the name was built originally for the United States Navy, as the destroyer *USS Philip*, but was transferred to the Royal Navy and commissioned in 1940. She escorted convoys between the Thames and the Forth and was once involved in the hazardous Russian Convoys of the Second World War. Finally she was a target ship for dive-bombing attacks in the Moray Firth.

In July 1993, the crew of the latest ship marched through the streets of Lancaster to gain the freedom of the city.

HMS LANCASTER

Built by Yarrow Shipbuilders Ltd, Scotstoun, Glasgow for the Royal Navy
Launched on 24 May 1990
Displacement – 3,500 tonnes; Length – 436.4 feet; Beam — 49.2 feet; Speed — 28 knots

HMS HOWE

Though *HMS Howe* was launched from Fairfield's shipyard in 1940 she didn't sail until 1942 and therefore gained the benefit of early experience in the Second World War. She carried better radar equipment and anti-aircraft armament.

The *Howe* was immediately attached to the Home Fleet and spent the first part of her career on the dramas of escorting supply ships on those notorious runs from the north of Scotland to Murmansk. The story of those Russian Convoys, helping the Soviets to fight the Nazis, became legend and was graphically described by Alistair MacLean in his famous first novel, *HMS Ulysses*.

The Howe's earlier sister ship, the *Prince of Wales*, had survived the encounter with Germany's "unsinkable" battleship, the *Bismarck*, which sank the Clyde-built *Hood* before she herself was pursued and sunk. The *Prince of Wales* later perished in an air attack while trying to prevent a Japanese landing on Malaya.

Back safely from the Russian adventure, the *Howe* set sail for Gibraltar and the invasion of Sicily, also taking part in the surrender of the Italian fleet in September 1943. She took over Taranto Harbour, one of Italy's major fleet anchorages.

In an overhaul at Devonport, the *Howe's* anti-aircraft armament was further increased and other changes included the extensive use of air-conditioning, an advantage for the tropical service to come.

She joined the Far East Fleet at Trincomalee in Ceylon, which became the principal British naval base in that part of the world after the fall of Singapore.

She joined the assembling fleet in Sydney, Australia, and in the spring of 1945 was part of Task Force 57, participating in the bombardment of Miyoko. Her anti-aircraft battery brought down one of Japan's kamikaze attackers.

With the war over, the *Howe* underwent an overhaul in Durban and after visits to Mombasa and Singapore made her way back to Britain, where she joined the Training Squadron at Portland.

After a comparatively short life she was ordered to be scrapped and in 1958 was towed to Inverkeithing, where she was broken up by T W Ward and Co. What did survive was the *Howe's* bell, which was presented by the Royal Navy to St Giles Cathedral in Edinburgh.

HMS HOWE
Built by Fairfields, Govan, Glasgow for the Royal Navy
Launched in August 1942
Displacement – 36,750 tons; Length – 745 feet; Beam – 103 feet; Speed – 28 knots

HMS HOOD

The particular pride of Clydebank in 1918 was the launching of what was indisputably the biggest warship in the world. The mighty *Hood* took her name from the Vice Admiral who was killed when the *Invincible* exploded at the Battle of Jutland and was launched by his widow, Lady Hood, as the First World War drew to a close.

Sadly, she would be remembered more for her end than her beginning. The fate of *HMS Hood* was one of the truly tragic tales of the Second World War.

In May 1941, she sailed with the *HMS Prince of Wales* from Scapa Flow, in the Orkneys, to join the hunt for the dreaded *Bismarck*, Germany's newest and fastest battleship which was declared to be unsinkable.

Catching up with her in the Denmark Strait, they engaged her in battle. Alas, in two minutes of high explosive action, a salvo from the *Bismarck* struck the *Hood's* ammunition magazine and the explosion burst the ship in two. She sank with unbelievable haste – and there were only three survivors from a crew of 1400.

After one of the Navy's blackest days, all else was dropped as the combined might of the fleet went in pursuit of the *Bismarck*. They caught her 550 miles west of Land's End and didn't rest till Germany's "unsinkable" ship was at the bottom of the Atlantic.

Arguments raged as to whether the *Hood* had been over-rated as the most massive and powerful of warships. After all, in view of the lessons of the Battle of Jutland, she had been given 5000 tons of extra protection.

Perhaps the most rational view came from retired Admiral of the Fleet Lord Chatfield, whose letter to The Times was surprisingly uncensored. The *Hood* was destroyed, he pointed out, because she had to fight a ship which was 22 years more modern than herself. For that, he blamed those who opposed the rebuilding of the British Battle Fleet until 1937.

The *Hood* had actually been due for reconstruction in 1939 but the outbreak of the Second World War prevented that.

In the 21 years since she left John Brown's yard, however, she had had her moments. As early as 1921, when the *Hood* was visiting Rosyth, she found herself caught up in the rail and coal strike. Her captain was ordered to prepare patrols to protect essential services if necessary.

The sailors were deployed at Cowdenbeath where miners were rioting. In an atmosphere described as "Bolshevik", there were attempts at sabotage. But the crew of the *Hood* had their own way of defusing the situation: They challenged the men to a football match.

On the lighter side the *Hood,* which also took part in the notorious Invergordon Mutiny, was to figure in a world cruise along with *HMS Repulse*.

But in July 1940 she took part in one of the most agonising of exercises – destroying a large part of the French Fleet (our own allies) to prevent it falling into German hands after the debacle of Dunkirk. Winston Churchill expressed regret at the loss of 1000 French sailors.

Ten months later the *Hood* was to meet her own tragic fate.

HMS HOOD

Built by John Brown & Company, Clydebank for the Royal Navy
Launched on 22 August 1918
Displacement – 46,200 tons; Length – 860.7 feet; Beam – 105.2 feet; Speed – 31 knots

QSS QUEEN MARY

Even if I had never sailed on the *Queen Mary* I suspect I would still be lauding her as the greatest ship that ever graced the ocean. To have crossed to New York on her third last voyage in 1967 was merely to confirm the opinion.

For here was the craftsmanship of the Clyde at its best, moulded into a majestic liner with the opulence of the most luxurious hotel you could have imagined.

Whether joining in the bustle of the bars, dancing in the magnificent main lounge with its Palm Court atmosphere, strolling on deck in the moonlight or answering the call of the church bells on the Sunday morning, you were savouring an exquisite experience which would linger for the rest of your life.

Yet the *Queen Mary's* beginnings were hardly auspicious. Having planned a weekly transatlantic service, Cunard needed two large ships. In anticipation of the order – and amid much secrecy in a back room of John Brown's shipyard at Clydebank – two young naval architects set to work on the specifications of the first ship. By coincidence, one of them was called John Brown, the man who has written the foreword to this book.

The design complete, work began in May 1930 but had to be suspended when Cunard faced the hazards of the Depression. But fresh money was raised for her completion and she was finally launched by Queen Mary on 26 September 1934. She sailed on her maiden voyage to New York in May 1936, stirring pride in her native Scotland thereafter when cinema newsreels would show her returning to Southampton with the rich and famous among her passengers.

Soon she had wrested the Blue Riband for the Atlantic crossing from the French ship *Normandie*. But in August 1939 she sailed for New York carrying many Americans escaping the threat of war in Europe. By March 1940 the *Queen Mary* was on her way to Sydney to become a troopship, a role she fulfilled throughout the Second World War, carrying 15,000 men at a time to encounters like the Battle of Alamein.

Winston Churchill was among her wartime passengers. Restored to peacetime purpose by 1947, the *Queen Mary* would spend the next twenty years criss-crossing the Atlantic with her sister ship, the *Queen Elizabeth*. Not best suited for the flexibility of cruising, however, she was running up financial loss by the 1960s, when Cunard set a date for her demise.

Into her final days, the *Queen Mary* sailed with dignity past the Statue of Liberty and onward to the Hudson River. As Manhattan beckoned through the morning mists, we stood in silence by her bows and remembered her illustrious past. She was sold to the City of Long Beach, California in 1967 and there she lies to this day, a hotel and tourist attraction, costly to maintain but treasured by a loyal band of admirers who have secured a form of "listed" status for the great lady – a true aristocrat of the Clyde.

QSS QUEEN MARY
Built by John Brown & Company, Clydebank for the Cunard White Star Line
Launched on 26 September 1934
Gross tonnage – 81,237; Length – 1,019.5 feet; Beam – 118.58 feet; Speed – 28.5 knots

QSS QUEEN ELIZABETH

If the great *Queen Mary* had to share top billing among the finest ships ever built, she would have to look no further than her younger sister, *Queen Elizabeth*. For 20 years after the war those two Cunarders plied the Atlantic as reminders of what that pre-war level of luxury really meant.

They had been conceived 20 years earlier by Sir Percy Bates, chairman of Cunard, but first the *Mary's* building had been interrupted by the Depression and then the Second World War delayed the peacetime role of the *Elizabeth* until 10 years after her keel was laid in 1936.

When it came to the *Elizabeth*, Dr John Brown, who had been involved in the design of the *Mary*, was in charge of the drawing office at the Clydebank yard of his namesake. (Happily, Dr Brown survives to write the foreword to this book). Refinement of design meant they could reduce the funnels from three to two.

The *Elizabeth* was launched in September 1938 by the lady who gave her name to the ship (known to later generations as the Queen Mother). Just before the naming ceremony there was a crash of timbers and the impatient lady moved off. Fortunately, the Queen had the presence of mind to cut the ribbon which released the bottle – and named the *Queen Elizabeth* only seconds before she was out of reach!

No such public ceremony attended her eventual departure in February 1940 when, with the onset of Hitler's war, she had to steal quietly across the Atlantic to join the *Queen Mary* in New York. Now she was a troopship, carrying up to 15,000 on such routes as Sydney to the Middle East. When the Japs threatened Australia, she carried American troops to Sydney. That war service had covered 500,000 miles, carrying more than 800,000 people.

On 16 October 1946, eight years after her launch, she finally sailed on that maiden passenger voyage to New York. That would be her main function for 22 years, carrying up to 2200 people, ranging from Winston Churchill to Charlie Chaplin, Bing Crosby and Bob Hope.

Both *Queens* lost money on cruising and soon after the *Mary* ended her service in 1967, Cunard sold the *Elizabeth* to an American company. She was then sold on to a Far East shipowner, C Y Tung, and renamed the Seawise University. But the concept of a floating university was never fulfilled.

On 9 January 1972, a number of fires were seen burning as she lay in Hong Kong Harbour and she eventually capsized. As a boy I had seen the *Elizabeth* in her cradle at Clydebank. Now I was hiring a boat to visit her graveyard in Hong Kong. Without doubt, arsonists had been at work. There she lay pathetically on her side – one of the saddest sights of a lifetime.

QSS QUEEN ELIZABETH
Built by John Brown & Co, Clydebank for the Cunard White Star Line
Launched on 27 September 1938
Gross tonnage – 83,673; Length – 1,031 feet; Beam – 118.4 feet; Speed – 28.5 knots

TSS QUEEN ELIZABETH 2

If the *Queen Mary* and *Queen Elizabeth* were essentially luxury liners of the 1930s, their young sister was unmistakably a child of the Swinging Sixties.

While the boilers of the *Mary* required three funnels and those of the *Elizabeth* required two, the design of the *QE2* was refined to a single funnel, a distinctive appendage which fitted well into the general elegance of Cunard's most recent royal lady.

Whereas her predecessors were conceived with the Atlantic in mind, the *QE2* had to be adaptable for the cruising purpose which would take up a considerable part of her year, as a commercial necessity.

By the time she was launched in September 1967, the old John Brown yard at Clydebank was in the process of becoming part of the newly-created Upper Clyde Shipbuilders. In the same month the dowager *Queen Mary* was making her very last triumphant crossing to New York.

After the speculation of what the new ship might be called, the final choice of *Queen Elizabeth 2* caused fresh rumblings among those who had disputed the historical accuracy of the Queen's title when she succeeded her father in 1952.

But there were even louder rumblings when the ship, now contracted in name to the *QE2*, developed blade failures in both turbines during trials and Cunard refused to accept her.

All was well, however, by the maiden voyage which took place from Southampton to New York on 2 May 1969.

If the grand opulence of those pre-war days was not so much in evidence, here was still a luxurious ship in the modern manner. She carries 564 first class passengers and 1441 tourist on the Atlantic run but cuts back to 1400 passengers with one class only for cruising..

With four plush restaurants, eight bars, theatre, casino and so many activities, the problem on these luxury liners is how to fit it all in. The crew of around 1000 include 100 chefs, 27 musicians, six dancers, two doctors, 13 hairdressers and a bell-boy.

The *QE2* has not been without incident. In 1971 she rescued passengers from the French liner *Antilles* which perished in the Caribbean. After a bomb threat in 1972, experts dropped in by parachute. A hoaxer was later arrested in New York.

Most unexpected of all, the *QE2* found herself caught up in the Falklands War of 1982. She carried 3000 troops to South Georgia and brought home survivors from the frigates *HMS Antelope* and *HMS Ardent* and the destroyer *HMS Coventry* which had been sunk.

Though the early turbine problems were cured, it was decided to reduce fuel costs. So in 1986 she was taken to Bremerhaven and converted to a diesel-electric ship.

Marking Cunard's 150th anniversary in 1990, the *QE2* undertook 22 cruises, from the Norwegian fjords to the Mediterranean and the Caribbean.